Wild Weather

WORLD
BOOK

www.worldbook.com

World Book, Inc.
180 North LaSalle Street
Suite 900
Chicago, Illinois 60601
USA

For information about other World Book publications,
visit our website at www.worldbook.com or call
1-800-WORLDBK (967-5325).

For information about sales to schools and libraries,
call 1-800-975-3250 (United States), or 1-800-837-5365
(Canada).

Library of Congress Cataloging-in-Publication Data for
this volume has been applied for.

This edition: ISBN: 978-0-7166-4059-2 (hc.)
ISBN: 978-0-7166-4056-1 (set, hc.)

Also available as: ISBN: 978-0-7166-4065-3 (e-book)

Printed in China by Shenzhen Wing King Tong Paper
Products Co., Ltd., Shenzhen, Guangdong
1st printing July 2018

Produced for World Book by
White-Thomson Publishing Ltd

www.wtpub.co.uk

Author: Paul Harrison
Editor: Izzi Howell
Design/Art director: Claire Gaukrodger
Illustrator: Rob Davis/The Art Agency

Cover artwork: © Doug Holgate

Staff

Executive Committee

President
Jim O'Rourke

Vice President and
Editor in Chief
Paul A. Kobasa

Vice President, Finance
Donald D. Keller

Vice President, Marketing
Jean Lin

Vice President, International
Sales
Maksim Rutenberg

Vice President, Technology
Jason Dole

Director, Human Resources
Bev Ecker

Editorial

Director, New Print
Tom Evans

Managing Editor
Jeff De La Rosa

Librarian
S. Thomas Richardson

Manager, Contracts &
Compliance
(Rights & Permissions)
Loranne K. Shields

Manager, Indexing Services
David Pofelski

Digital

Director, Digital Product
Development
Erika Meller

Manager, Digital Products
Jonathan Wills

Graphics and Design

Senior Art Director
Tom Evans

Senior Web Designer/Digital
Media Developer
Matt Carrington

Manufacturing/Production

Manufacturing Manager
Anne Fritzinger

Proofreader
Nathalie Strassheim

A glossary of terms appears on p. 94.

Contents

Zac Newton and friends

Zac is a junior genius and inventor of the Backspace app. The app allows Zac and his friends to take virtual trips through time and space, just by snapping a selfie.

Lucía has a sharp mind and an even sharper wit. She pretends to be too cool for school, but inside she burns to learn about science.

Quick-thinking Marcus is always ready with a joke. Although he loves to clown around, he knows more than he lets on.

Ning likes to run, jump, and play ball. She may be the youngest of the group, but nobody's going to push her around.

Zac's dog, Orbit, loves to join Zac and his friends on their adventures. He's not afraid of anything—except loud noises.

Chapter 1
Storm Warning

"That is one big cloud!" said Lucía, pointing at an enormous white cloud approaching from the south. The cloud reached high into the blue sky. At its top, the cloud flattened and spread outward.

"It looks kind of like a giant mushroom," said Ning.

"Actually, it's a cumulonimbus," said Zac Newton.

"*KYOO myuh loh*-what?" frowned Lucía.

"A big name for a big cloud!" smiled Marcus. "Like I told you, everything's big here in Oklahoma."

Marcus spread out his arms, taking in the vast landscape that surrounded him, Ning, Lucía, and Zac. Yellow prairie grass stretched in every direction, as far as the eye could see.

Marcus's parents had sent him to the Oklahoma countryside to spend the week visiting his Aunt Kim and cousin, Jayden. Best of all, Aunt Kim had let him bring his friends along.

Zac's dog, Orbit, barked nervously at the cloud.

"It's alright, Orbit," said Lucía, leaning down to scratch the dog's head. "It may be big and have a super long name, but it can't hurt you."

"I wouldn't be too sure about that," said a voice behind them. They turned to see Marcus's cousin Jayden coming out the back door of the house. Jayden was a tall young man in his early 20's.

"How can a cumulo-thingamajig hurt us, Jay?" asked Marcus.

"It's called a cumulonimbus," Jayden corrected him. "And, it can produce a thunderstorm—or worse!"

"Worse than a thunderstorm?" asked Ning, squinting up at the cloud. "What exactly are we talking about?"

Jayden smiled. "We're talking about tornadoes."

"That cloud can make a tornado?" gasped Marcus.

"Possibly." Jayden nodded. "And, if it does, you can bet I'll be chasing it."

Marcus beamed with pride. His cousin had studied weather science in college—meteorology, he called it. Now he worked as a storm chaser. "We're coming too, right, Jay?" asked Marcus.

"No way!" laughed Jayden. "It's far too dangerous for you kids." Jayden could see that Marcus was disappointed, so he added, "Tell you what, though, I'll show you the vehicle I drive when I chase tornadoes, or twisters, as we sometimes call them. I named my vehicle Shango, after a storm god in African mythology. It's pretty impressive!"

Jayden popped back into the house to grab his keys. Then, they all started down the long path that led to the garage.

"Do you get many tornadoes around here?" Zac asked Jayden as the group walked.

"More than almost any place on Earth," Jayden said proudly. "We get around 60 tornadoes a year in Oklahoma. The biggest ones are the most exciting and terrifying things you'll ever see. The winds inside a twister can swirl at over 300 miles per hour. That's almost 500 kilometers per hour, if you're into metric measurements. I've seen them lift a car into the air."

As he talked, Jayden kept glancing up at the giant cloud above. Its bottom had grown much darker in the last five minutes, and the wind had begun to pick up.

"The most dangerous tornadoes form out of a kind of thunderstorm called a *supercell*," he told them. "What I see up there in the sky right now could be the start of a supercell. I'll have to move fast if a tornado forms. They can be pretty tough to follow."

"Why's that?" asked Ning. She hunched her shoulders against the growing wind.

"Well, in general, they move the same direction as the rest of the storm. But tornadoes can be very unpredictable, swerving first one way, then another. A tornado can be in front of you one minute, and right behind you the next…"

"Kind of like Orbit," said Lucía, pointing at the dog. Orbit was darting excitedly back and forth, chasing a tumbleweed that blew along the path.

"Yeah, exactly like Orbit!" laughed Jayden.

By now, the wind was whistling in their ears, and they had to shout to hear one another. The sky had turned

darker, and hailstones began to fall.

"I hate storms!" groaned Marcus. "And these
hailstones are big! Ouch!"

"Like you said—everything is big in Oklahoma!"
smirked Lucía.

Marcus did not laugh. "I want out of here!" he whined.

"Let's run!" shouted Jayden. The six of them sprinted
the final few steps to the garage. The children sheltered

against the building while Jayden unlocked the door.

"What makes these hailstones so big?" wondered Ning, rubbing her arm where one had struck her.

"Hailstones start off as tiny frozen raindrops inside a thundercloud," Zac told her. "These frozen pellets tend to fall toward the ground. As they fall, however, they meet air currents called *updrafts*."

"Updrafts?" asked Marcus. "I guess they're called that because the air is blowing upward, right?"

"Right," Zac agreed. "If the updrafts aren't too strong, the tiny pellets will continue falling to the ground. But if the updrafts are powerful enough, they'll whip the pellets back up into the cloud. There, droplets of water and particles of ice continue to freeze around them, making them bigger and bigger. Eventually, the hailstone gets so big and heavy that it breaks through the updrafts and falls to the ground."

"I've seen hailstones as big as grapefruits," said Jayden. "Believe me, you do not want to get hit by one of those."

He slid open the garage door. Everyone gasped at the sight of the vehicle inside. "Meet Shango," Jayden announced. Shango, the children guessed, had once been an ordinary four-wheel-drive truck. Now, it was covered in so much armor that it looked more like a tank.

"Shango is protected by thick plates of steel welded to a frame of steel tubing," explained Jayden. "Fully loaded, Shango weighs almost as much as a school bus. Even so, the turbocharged diesel engine has enough power to give it a top speed of 100 miles—that's 160 kilometers—per hour. So, Shango can keep up with those twisters, and—if necessary—get away from them!"

"What about the windows?" asked Ning.

"Bulletproof glass," smiled Jayden.

As the others talked, Lucía peered through Shango's rear windows. She saw something odd inside. It was a short, flat cone of metal painted orange. Its base was a circle little bigger than a dinner plate. She was about to ask Jayden what it was when Shango began beeping loudly.

"What's that noise?" cried Marcus.

Jayden flung open the driver's side door. He checked a flashing screen on the console. "The radar's picked up a signal," he said. His eyes grew wide with excitement. "I was right! A tornado has formed just south of here." Then he let out a gasp. "It's... hey, it's an EF3! My first one! I have to get after it!"

He leapt inside the vehicle and started the engine. "Sorry, kids, there's no time to lose!"

"But are you sure we..." Marcus began as Shango roared to life. "... can't come with?" he finished sadly, as the truck sped away.

The friends ran out of the garage. The hailstorm had stopped, but the wind was still howling. The daylight had turned a strange yellow color. They watched Shango speeding into the distance.

Then they looked beyond, to where the truck was headed, and they witnessed a sight that none of them would ever forget.

Chapter 2
A Windy Debate

The big white cloud they had seen before had become a dark, swirling, bowl-shaped monster. It seemed to fill most of the sky. Lightning flashed deep inside the cloud every now and then. Suddenly, a twisting cone of air seemed to grow from the cloud's bottom. The cone's tip moved downward, whirling closer and closer to the ground. When it finally touched down, a great cloud of dust flew up around it.

Marcus gulped nervously. He watched the distant Shango speeding toward the vicious, twisting tornado. "You know," he said to the others, "maybe it's a good thing that Jayden left us behind."

For several minutes, the children continued to stare at the tornado. It disappeared into the distance. Shango followed carefully behind. The wind began to die down, and the weather—at least where they were—grew calmer.

"Do you think Jayden will be okay?" said Lucía.

"I'm sure he'll be fine," said Marcus. "He's a professional."

"All this excitement has made me hungry," said Ning.

"Me, too," said Marcus. "Let's go rustle up some lunch."

Orbit barked in agreement, and the five of them started back up the path.

When they reached the house, they found Aunt Kim in the living room. Aunt Kim was a short woman, with long braids and large hoop earrings. Just then, she was staring at the screen of a laptop computer. She wore headphones and was speaking into a microphone attached to a radio. Aunt Kim looked up as the children entered. She greeted them with a big, welcoming smile.

"I've been talking to Jay," she told them. "The twister's been on the ground for almost 10 minutes now. He's been streaming some unbelievable video! Come see."

The children gathered around her and gazed at the laptop screen. It showed close-up video of the churning, whirling brown cloud. As they watched, a telephone pole near the twister snapped like a twig.

"That's close enough, Jay!" Aunt Kim scolded into the microphone.

The children couldn't hear Jayden's reply, but they were relieved to see Aunt Kim's smile grow more relaxed. "I know you're a professional, my boy, but you can't stop a mother from worrying." She turned around. "Go help yourself to some food, kids. There's chicken-fried steak and sweet corn in the kitchen. I'll come and join you in a little while."

A few minutes later, the children were sitting at the kitchen table eating. Ning was the first to speak up. "I wish I understood what a tornado is and how tornadoes happen."

"Maybe we should try asking a few experts," said Zac, chewing thoughtfully on some corn. He pulled out his cell phone and tapped the screen a few times. "I know someone who can tell us about clouds and storms. That would be a start, wouldn't it?"

"Are we going to use your Backspace app?" asked Lucía excitedly. The Backspace app was Zac's greatest invention. It could take Zac and his friends on a virtual visit to any time or place in history, all without really leaving the present.

"That's the plan!" said Zac. "You remember how it works?"

The friends quickly finished their meals and gathered around Zac. He held out his phone at arm's length, preparing to take a group selfie. "Make sure you can all see yourselves on the screen," said Zac. "We don't want to leave anybody behind!"

They all squeezed in a little closer, and Zac pressed the button.

FLASH!

ZUMMMMMM
mmmmmmm...

There was a bright
flash that made the
children squint. When it
faded, the scene around them
had changed. Aunt Kim's kitchen
was gone, and they were standing
in a lecture hall. Rows of seats faced a
central stage.

The seats were full of men in dark coats and shirts
with stiff, high collars. They were listening with interest
to a short, silver-haired man standing onstage. As he
spoke, he sketched on a chalkboard, illustrating his
ideas.

"Who is that man?" asked Ning.

"That's James Pollard Espy," said Zac. "He's been
called the Storm King. He was the leading expert on
storms in his day."

"What day is that?" asked Marcus.

"The mid-1800's. Here he is in Philadelphia, Pennsylvania, in 1842, giving a talk to a group of scientists. Let's listen in on what he has to say."

"So, you see," Espy was explaining to the audience, "when the sun warms the air, the air rises. This air contains water vapor...."

"Excuse me?" said Lucía, putting up her hand.

Espy turned. He was surprised to see four children and a dog sharing the stage with him. "Ah, some late arrivals!" he said. "And how can I help you?"

"I was just wondering what water vapor is," said Lucía.

"An excellent question," smiled Espy. "Water vapor is water in the form of a gas. Have you felt humid air?"

"Yes!" Lucía answered, thinking of the hottest, stickiest summer day she could remember.

"Humidity is the result of water vapor in the air. Now,

as warm air rises, it gradually cools. The water vapor starts to condense..."

"Um..." began Ning, putting up her hand.

Espy turned to the children once again. "Yes, how can I help?"

"What does condense mean?" asked Ning.

"Another brilliant question!" said Espy. "To condense means to change from a gas into a liquid or solid. As I was saying, as the air rises, it cools. As it cools, the water vapor condenses into little droplets of liquid water and particles of ice floating in the air. These droplets and particles are what make up clouds."

"Thank you," said Ning.

Espy turned back to the audience. "When water vapor condenses, it gives off heat, creating an area of low atmospheric pressure. The low pressure sucks in surrounding air. The air rushes in from all directions to a central point, where the pressure is lowest. We feel this rush of air as wind. If the pressure is low enough, a storm can result..."

"Balderdash!" cried a voice from the audience. Everyone turned to see who had interrupted. A tall, thin man with a shock of white hair had risen from his seat in the fourth row.

"What a rude man!" remarked Lucía. "Who is he?"

"That's William Charles Redfield," said Zac. "He's Espy's greatest rival. The two men hate each other."

Redfield pointed a long, bony finger at Espy. "You, sir, are a phony!"

"Unlike you, I've seen storms," continued Redfield. "I've seen the way that trees and cornstalks are blown down in a spiral shape. Wind doesn't rush in toward a central point, as you describe. It rotates, I tell you! Wind rotates!"

Espy turned red with anger. "How dare you interrupt my lecture with your silly ideas!" he bellowed. "Rotating storms? What bunkum! My experiments clearly show…"

"Your experiments?" laughed Redfield. "You should try stepping out of the laboratory once in a while, sir! Get out there in the wind and rain. You'll see what storms do. You'll see they're just like whirlpools, but in the air rather than the water."

Espy's eyes bulged with fury. His fists were clenched. He looked like he wanted to thump Redfield on the nose.

"This is getting a little stormy!" joked Marcus.

"It's probably time we got out of here," said Zac, tapping the screen of his phone. The virtual world disappeared, and they were back in Aunt Kim's kitchen.

"So who was right, Espy or Redfield?" asked Ning.

"They were both right and both wrong," said Zac. "Espy was right about what causes storms, but he was wrong about how winds behave. Redfield was right that storm winds rotate, but he was wrong to deny Espy's ideas about pressure. Still, their argument was useful. It helped people to better understand storms."

"So scientific progress isn't always just about some genius working alone," said Lucía.

"Yeah, sometimes what science needs is a fight!" chuckled Marcus, holding up his fists.

Zac gave him a stern look.

Marcus quickly added, "By fight, of course, I mean a lively debate."

Chapter 3
Front Page News

The radio on the kitchen counter was playing country music. The song was interrupted by an announcer, who broke in to deliver a severe weather warning.

"Hey, the announcer just mentioned this area," said Lucía.

The children turned their attention to the radio. The announcer gave an update on the tornado Jayden was chasing. The announcer also warned of more severe storms, damaging winds, and large hail expected throughout the area. The public was strongly advised to stay indoors.

"Don't worry, we will!" said Marcus.

"How do they know?" Ning suddenly asked.

"Know what?" asked Zac.

"What to expect with the weather," said Ning. "I mean, they're predicting the future, aren't they? No one can do that."

"In a way, they are predicting the future." Zac nodded. "And, for a very long time, no one could. Before about a hundred years ago, most weather forecasting was a mixture of guesswork and superstition. People had sayings like 'Red sky at night, sailor's delight,' that kind of thing."

"What does that mean?" asked Ning.

"It means that if you see a reddish glow in the sky around sunset, clear weather is on the way," explained Zac. "It was a saying people used to try to predict the weather. That was back when they didn't really understand what caused weather."

"So what changed?" asked Lucía.

"People started studying the weather in a more scientific way, trying to work out what causes it," Zac explained. "Two people from Norway did more than anyone to turn weather forecasting into a science. They were Vilhelm Bjerknes—pronounced *bih AIRK nehs*— and his son Jacob."

"Ooh, could we meet them?" urged Lucía. "I've

always wanted to visit Norway, even if it is only a virtual trip."

"I think that I can arrange that," said Zac, studying his phone. "Gather around. I'll take you back to 1918, when Jacob had a flash of inspiration."

FLASH!

ZUMMMMMMmmmmmmmm...

The scene suddenly changed. They were standing outside a log cabin. It was perched on top of a high cliff, overlooking a narrow inlet of the sea.

"Cool valley!" said Marcus.

"It's called a fjord," explained Lucía, sounding it out for them, "*fyawrd*. There's a *j* in it, but it sounds like a *y*. We learned about fjords in geography. Norway has tons of them."

Through the cabin's doorway, they could see two men, both tall and lean. The older one sat in an armchair reading a newspaper. The younger one stared out the window at the sky over the fjord.

Suddenly, the young man, Jacob, turned to his father. "Father, I've been thinking about the boundaries where masses of cold air and masses of warm air meet."

"Just the sort of thing I say to my dad all the time," joked Marcus.

Jacob turned to the doorway in surprise. Vilhelm looked up from his paper.

"Hello!" Jacob said to Marcus. "Do you and your

friends want to come in out of the cold?"

The children and Orbit crowded into the cabin.

"Are you and your father also interested in the weather, young man?" Vilhelm asked Marcus.

Marcus stammered, "N-No… I mean, I was kidding. We never talk like that."

"What my friend means," said Zac, turning to Jacob, "is that we'd all really like to hear your ideas, sir."

Jacob nodded and continued, "Well, we know there are often storms, high winds, and rain where warm air masses meet cool air masses, but we don't yet know why."

"No, we don't," agreed Vilhelm. "I suspect you have a theory, though, Jac. Am I right?"

Jacob placed his hands opposite each other as if he was about to start clapping. "Imagine my hands are the two air masses meeting each other," he said.

Then he tilted his hands, so both were diagonal, but still parallel. "We know from the work you've already done, Father, that the air masses slope like this when they meet. The cold air mass is below, and the warm air mass is above. The warm air rises along this slope, and the cold air sinks, like so."

Jacob moved his left hand diagonally upward while moving his right one diagonally down. "Do you see how this movement could produce the energy needed to create cyclones?"

"Cyclones?" frowned Lucía.

"Cyclones are winds that spin around an area of low atmospheric pressure," Jacob explained.

Jacob thought for a moment, then grabbed a pencil from the table. He held it between his slanted hands. "Imagine this pencil is a column of air caught between the two air masses." Jacob slid his hands past each other again. The pencil spun between them. "As the air masses move, the air column swirls, just as this pencil twirls, forming a cyclone. Cyclones develop along the

boundary between air masses, causing storms and so on."

"It's a very interesting idea, and one we ought to study further," nodded Vilhelm. "We'll need a name for these boundaries between air masses—something that will help people to picture them."

Jacob spotted a headline in the newspaper in his father's lap. It was a report about the progress of the first World War, which was being fought in Europe at that time. The headline read "Allied armies push Germans back on Western Front."

"How about calling them fronts?" said Jacob.

Vilhelm smiled. "Fronts… like the battle lines between opposing armies. It's perfect!"

The scene faded to white, and a second later, the children were back in Aunt Kim's kitchen.

Zac finished the story. "Jacob, Vilhelm, and others continued to work on Jacob's theory. They figured out how these cyclones form, grow, and die out. All of that helped to make weather forecasts possible. And Jacob's name for the boundaries where air masses meet stuck— we still call them *weather fronts* today."

"That was all very interesting," said Ning. "But I still don't understand what causes a tornado."

"The honest truth is that even now, scientists aren't sure exactly how tornadoes form," said Zac. "But I'll try to explain what we do know." He grabbed a pad and pen from the kitchen counter and began sketching a diagram.

"As Espy said, the condensation of moisture in rising air releases heat, lowering atmospheric pressure. This low pressure drags air into the bottom of the cloud, forming updrafts. In a supercell storm, the updrafts are really powerful. They move around inside the cloud. Sometimes the winds high up move faster or slower than the ones lower down. This difference in speed causes the column of rising air to spin, much like Jacob's pencil did. This is called a mesocyclone…"

"Mesocyclone?" interrupted Marcus. "Is that like the cyclones Jacob was talking about?"

"It's similar," said Zac. "Like those cyclones, it's a spinning mass of air around an area of low pressure. But a mesocyclone is much smaller. You need one more thing to make a tornado, and that's a wall cloud."

"What's a wall cloud?" asked Lucía.

"It's a low, dark, heavy cloud that forms beneath the mesocyclone. The tornado grows from the bottom of the wall cloud."

"Sounds like a lot needs to happen before you can get a tornado," said Ning. "That's probably why they're quite rare."

"Not rare enough," muttered Marcus.

Chapter 4

Tornado Tracks

Outside, the winds were picking up again. Heavy rain began splattering against the kitchen window. Orbit woofed nervously.

"I hope the tornado hasn't decided to turn around and head back this way," said Marcus with a shiver. "Or, maybe this is the start of another one. I wish I knew." He tried tuning the radio to different stations, but he couldn't find another weather report.

"I'm glad that those Norwegian guys did a lot for weather forecasting," Marcus muttered. "But, it's one thing to say it might rain tomorrow—I'm guessing it's a lot harder to predict something that develops really quickly, like a tornado."

"You may be right about that," said Zac. "Although, it hasn't stopped people from trying." He began thumbing the touchscreen of his phone. "It all started with a guy named John Park Finley…"

FLASH!

ZUMMMMMMmmmmmmm...

The friends were transported to a bleak, flat landscape with barely a tree or bush in sight. They were standing in a shallow brown trench. The trench wound through the grassy plain like a dry riverbed. Inside it, the grass lay flattened, twisted, and dead.

"I do not like this place," said Marcus.

"Where and when are we?" asked Lucía.

"Nebraska, 1879," said Zac.

"I thought we were going to meet Mr. Finley," said Ning.

"Yeah, so did I." Zac frowned. "I hope we haven't missed him."

Marcus looked at a flattened bush. "If this is the trail he leaves behind, I'm glad we missed him!"

"This must have been done by a tornado, silly!" Lucía smiled.

"There he is," said Zac. He pointed into the distance. A man in military uniform was walking toward them along the trench. Finley was a big man. He had rough skin and a mustache that made him look like a walrus.

"Howdy!" Finley said, when he reached the children. His eyebrows were raised in surprise. "What are you kids doing out here?"

"Everyone has to be somewhere," said Marcus.

"What are you doing here, sir?" Zac asked.

"Studying tornado tracks," replied Finley.

"That sounds interesting," said Ning. "Why are you doing that?"

Finley cleared his throat. "It is my view," he said, "that by studying tornado tracks like this one, we can learn more about these destructive winds. One day, we might even be able to predict when and where they'll strike. We'll be able to send out tornado warnings, helping to save many lives."

"That sounds cool!" said Marcus.

"The temperature of the tornado—whether cool or warm—is not something I can comment on, young man," said Finley. He was obviously confused by Marcus's choice of words. "However, I am convinced there is much we can learn about them."

"What have you learned so far?" Zac asked.

"I know that there are certain parts of the United States where tornadoes are more likely—the Great Plains and the Midwest, for example," Finley explained. "These places are where two different kinds of air meet. Warm, moist air blows north from a body of water called the Gulf of Mexico. Cool, dry air blows south from Canada. Where the two kinds of air meet, the atmosphere becomes unstable—that is, quick to change."

Finley continued, "I've made studies of the clouds, temperatures, and wind directions in these regions at the time of tornadoes. I've started to put together a set of rules that we can use to predict tornadoes. The army has agreed to give me some funding, so I can set up a forecasting service. Now, if you wouldn't mind, I must continue with my work."

With that, Finley stomped off along the tornado track.

"That sounds like good news," said Lucía as they watched him go. "So, did he start predicting tornadoes?"

"Let's jump forward eight years and find out," said Zac. "I'll put the app in 'secret observer' mode this time, so

Finley can't see or hear us. We don't want to scare him!"

Zac pushed another button, and the scene switched to an office. Finley stood with his head bowed, looking a little older. His commanding officer was seated behind a desk.

"I'm sorry, Sergeant Finley," the officer was saying. "We're closing down your tornado forecasting service."

"But why?" pleaded Finley. "We're having such success!"

"It's true, you've been very good at predicting when tornadoes won't strike. But, you're not so good at telling us when they will."

"We're improving all the time…"

"I'm sorry, the decision is final," said the officer. "Oh, and by the way, we're also banning the word *tornado* from weather forecasts. People get frightened when they hear it. From now on, we're calling them severe local storms."

Finley slouched from the room, defeated.

"I feel sorry for him," said Ning.

Zac nodded. "Yeah, this was bad news for John Finley and also for tornado science. For the next 60 years, research on tornadoes basically stopped. As you heard, weather forecasters weren't even allowed to use the word."

"So what happened 60 years later to change that?" asked Lucía.

"Let's take a look," said Zac, tapping the screen of his phone.

This time, as the flash faded, they found themselves standing in the middle of a ruined military base. In the evening shadows, they saw collapsed walls, broken roofs, and overturned vehicles.

The mournful wail of a siren came from somewhere nearby. Under the glare of emergency lighting, they watched an injured man being helped into an ambulance.

Men in United States Air Force uniforms wandered around, looking dazed. Strangely, many of them had smiles on their faces.

"This is Tinker Air Force Base, in Oklahoma, on the evening of March 25, 1948," said Zac. "About half an hour ago, a tornado blew through here."

"So then why is everybody smiling?" asked Marcus.

"Maybe they can explain," said Zac. He pointed out two officers who were walking slowly through the base. They, too, were looking cheerful.

"Excuse me," said Zac. "Could you explain why everyone's looking so happy?"

"Because this is a fantastic success!" one of them said. He turned to his companion. "Don't you agree, Captain Miller?"

"Absolutely, Major Fawbush!" beamed the other.

"What are you both talking about? This is a disaster!" Ning shouted.

"I wouldn't say that," said Fawbush, looking around. "Just a few minor injuries."

"It could have been so much worse," nodded Miller. "If it wasn't for our forecast, many of these people might be dead right now."

"You managed to forecast a tornado?" said Lucía. "That's amazing!"

"How did you know it was coming?" Zac asked.

"Well, five days ago, there was another tornado not

far from here," explained Fawbush. "We made a study of the weather at the time, writing down the wind speed and direction and the temperature."

"We looked for patterns to see what conditions might lead to a tornado," added Miller.

"This morning, we found those exact same conditions developing here, near this base," said Fawbush. "It seemed incredible that a tornado would strike this area again so soon. But we put our trust in the science, and sent out the warning."

"The tornado struck just after six o'clock, like we told them it would," said Miller. "By that time, they'd managed to get the aircraft into hangars and most of the people to safety."

Just then, one of the airmen came rushing up and saluted them. "On behalf of the m-men on the base," he stammered, "I'd just l-like to say that you two are heroes!"

"Why, thank you," said Fawbush. "I hope we've

proved that it is possible to forecast a tornado."

The air base faded as the children returned to the humble setting of Aunt Kim's kitchen.

"Fawbush and Miller's forecast was the first step in establishing a nationwide tornado warning service," said Zac.

Marcus looked out of the kitchen window. The sun was once again peeping through the clouds. In a stern voice, he announced, "The Marcus Tornado Warning Service forecasts no more tornadoes today, at least not here."

"How reassuring!" Lucía said to him. "And could you explain to me your methods, please, professor?"

Before Marcus could reply, Aunt Kim came in with an anxious look on her face. "I'm worried about Jayden," she said quietly. "I can't get hold of him on the radio."

Chapter 5

The Fujita Scale

"Jayden was talking to me when the radio suddenly cut out," Aunt Kim told the children. "The video stopped streaming at around the same time. I wish I'd asked him more about the tornado he was chasing. There are a lot of things he doesn't tell me, because he doesn't want me to worry. I'm afraid that this tornado may have been bigger and more dangerous than usual."

Aunt Kim looked at each of the children in turn. "Do you remember him saying anything when the alert came through—anything about what kind of a tornado it was?"

"He said it was an EF3," Ning recalled. "He seemed excited. He said it was his first one."

"An EF3?" Aunt Kim frowned.

"Do you know what that is, Auntie?" asked Marcus.

Aunt Kim shook her head.

Zac typed "EF3" into his phone and squinted at the screen. "It says here that the *F* stands for *Fujita*. It's a scale for measuring tornadoes. It is named for the great tornado scientist, Ted Fujita. But I don't know what the three means."

"Well, kids, your job is to find out what an EF3 is," said Aunt Kim. "Meanwhile, I'm going to the gas station to fill up the station wagon, in case I need to go out looking for Jayden."

When Aunt Kim had left, Zac began tapping away on his phone. "Who better to explain than Dr. Fujita himself?" He paused. "Okay, we're ready. Gather around."

When they were all in position, he pressed the Backspace button.

FLASH!

ZUMMMMMMmmmmmmm...

The next thing the children knew, they were in a laboratory. A Japanese American man stood before a strange-looking machine. It had a circular base. Rising up from that was a spinning, snaking whirlpool of vapor, like a miniature tornado.

"Now that's the size of tornado I can handle!" said Marcus.

The man appeared to be deep in thought. He didn't even hear Marcus or notice that he was no longer alone.

"That's Ted Fujita," whispered Zac. "It's May 1970, and he's about to have a big idea."

As Zac said this, Fujita suddenly burst into motion. He grabbed a pad and pen and began scribbling something down.

Ning wandered up to the miniature tornado, fascinated by its twisting shape. She reached out her hand to touch it, but drew it back when she felt an icy chill.

"Careful!" said Fujita.

"What is it?" Ning asked.

"It's a tornado simulator," he said, "a machine that makes a miniature whirlwind, like a model of a tornado. It helps me in my studies of these winds. We know so little about them. We don't even know how to compare one tornado to another."

Fujita shook the pad he'd been writing on. "I've just had this idea—wouldn't it be great if we could grade tornadoes by how strong they are, the way we do with earthquakes?"

"You mean like on a scale?" said Zac.

Fujita turned to him. "Yes, exactly. On a scale."

"So how would this scale work?" asked Ning.

Fujita looked at the notes he had made. "Well, we could call the weakest tornado a zero, and the most severe a five."

"So a three must be somewhere in the middle," Lucía whispered to Marcus.

"May I ask how exactly you plan to measure the strength of the tornadoes, sir?" Zac chimed in.

"That still needs to be worked out," replied Fujita, "but I imagine we'll look at things like estimated wind speed and the damage it would do if it hit a town or city. A zero on the scale, for example, would…"

They listened as Fujita worked through the details of his scale. A three on the scale, he thought, would describe tornadoes with winds up to 207 miles or 333 kilometers per hour, which could cause "severe damage." By severe damage, he meant roofs and walls torn off houses, trees snapped or uprooted, that kind of thing.

"That sounds pretty severe!" winced Marcus.

"I agree," said Zac grimly. With a few clicks of his phone, he returned them to the present.

"We should tell Aunt Kim," said Ning.

"There's one thing I don't get," said Marcus. "Jayden said the tornado was an EF3. If the F stands for Fujita, and the three is how strong the tornado is, what does the E stand for?"

"Good point," said Zac, typing away on his screen.

"According to this website, scientists changed the Fujita scale in 2007," said Zac. "By then, the scale had been in use for over 30 years. In all that time, scientists had learned much more about tornado damage and wind speeds. So they updated the scale. They called it the *Enhanced* Fujita Scale."

"There's the *E!*" shouted Marcus.

Zac continued, "It says here that EF3 tornadoes have wind speeds of 136 to 165 miles per hour. That's 219 to 266 kilometers per hour! These tornadoes cause 'severe damage.' They can destroy entire stories of well-built houses, severely damage large buildings, overturn trains, and lift heavy cars off the ground."

"A tornado can lift cars off the ground?" groaned Marcus. He thought of poor Jayden driving around in Shango.

Chapter 6
Trumpets on a Train

When Aunt Kim learned how powerful the tornado was and what it could do, her face became serious.

"Jayden may be in trouble," she said. "Perhaps he got too close and crashed. He could be injured somewhere. I have to go look for him."

"Can we come, too?" asked Ning and Lucía together.

Aunt Kim looked unsure. "I don't want to put you kids in any danger."

"I can help you track the storm," said Ning.

"And I can try to get a hold of Jayden on the radio while you drive," offered Lucía.

"And I can help with scientific advice," suggested Zac.

"And I can..." Marcus trailed off. All the important jobs had been taken.

"You can look after Orbit," said Lucía.

"Woof!" barked Orbit.

"All right, all right," said Aunt Kim, "you can all come, but we're not going near the tornado. Speaking of which, I guess it must have moved on by now. We'll need to find out where it went, so we know which way to look for Jayden."

Ning tapped the keys on Aunt Kim's laptop. "Internet access is down," she grumbled. "Storm damage, probably. That means we won't be able to track the tornado."

"There might be another way," said Aunt Kim. "Jayden has some sort of storm-tracking equipment in his bedroom. He calls it his, uh, Doppler radar. I'm not sure how it works, though."

The children raced upstairs with Orbit chasing after, leaving Aunt Kim behind. They found Jayden's bedroom a total mess. Scattered everywhere were clothes, books, magazines, and scientific instruments.

"This is just like your bedroom, Marcus!" teased Lucía.

"Tidiness runs in our family," Marcus joked.

On a desk in the corner sat a computer. It was connected to a series of black boxes with dials and switches on the front. A wire trailed from this equipment out the window to an antenna on the roof.

"That's the Doppler radar," said Zac.

"What's a Doppler radar?" asked Ning.

"To explain that, I first need to tell you about something called the Doppler effect," said Zac. "It was discovered in 1842 by a guy named Christian Doppler…"

"I sense more time travel approaching," smiled Lucía.

The children crowded around the phone.

FLASH!

ZUMMMMMMmmmmmmm...

The messy bedroom was replaced with a very different scene. The children were standing on a railway platform. Two men were also standing there, wearing long coats and top hats.

"The date is June 3, 1845," Zac announced. "We're in Holland, just outside the city of Utrecht. We're about to watch one of the most famous experiments in physics."

"Is that the one that proves time always moves slower when you're waiting for a train?" joked Marcus.

"No, it's the one that says Marcus will always try to be funny at the wrong moment," said Lucía.

"Shhh!" hissed Zac. "Can you hear that?"

The children listened. In the distance, they could hear the rattling wheels and clanking engine of an approaching steam train. But that wasn't all they heard. Above this sound came the distant blast of trumpets—lots of trumpets, all playing the same high note.

"Trumpets on a train?" asked Ning.

"Sounds like the name of a bad movie," said Marcus.

The noise of the locomotive and the brassy trumpets grew steadily louder. Finally, they saw it—an ancient-looking steam engine. Black smoke billowed from a chimney at the front of the locomotive as it clattered toward them along the track.

Orbit began barking ferociously, and Marcus had to calm him. The locomotive was pulling a flatbed car. Standing on the car were six trumpeters playing a single piercing note with all their might.

"There's something you don't see every day!" yelled Ning.

The two men on the platform grew excited at the approach of the train and the trumpeters. They began arguing among themselves.

"They're playing an E," said one.

"No, it's an E flat," said the other.

The train roared through the station without slowing. As it rushed passed them and began to move away again, a strange thing happened.

"The note that those trumpeters were playing just

went lower!" cried Lucía.

Everyone had noticed a slight deepening of the sound. This included the two gentlemen in top hats.

"Now they're playing an E flat," said one.

"No, it's a D," said the other.

"That's the Doppler effect," said Zac.

"What is the Doppler effect?" demanded Ning.

"What you just heard," laughed Zac. "Doppler discovered it three years earlier, but this was the first big experiment to test it out. And it worked! You all heard how the trumpet note changed, right?"

"Right!" said Marcus. "So Doppler proved that trumpeters can't hold a note while rushing along on a train. Big deal!"

"You don't understand," said Zac. "The trumpeters did hold the note. If you'd been on that train with them, you wouldn't have heard any difference. The note would have sounded exactly the same. But to us, standing here on the platform, it changed."

"Why?" asked Lucía.

"It's all about sound waves," said Zac. "Sound travels through the air in waves, something like waves in the ocean. The closer together the waves are, the higher the pitch of the sound. When a trumpeter plays a note, sound waves spread out evenly in all directions."

"Now think about the trumpeter in motion, on the train. As the train moves our way, the sound waves pile up in front of it. The waves get closer, making the trumpet sound more high-pitched. As the train passes and continues on, the sound waves get stretched out behind it. The waves become farther apart, making the pitch sound lower. That's the Doppler effect."

"Pretty neat!" said Marcus. "But how's that going to help us find a tornado?"

"I'm just getting to that," said Zac. The train station

faded, and they found themselves back in the mess of Jayden's room.

Zac waded through the clutter to the computer and turned it on. He continued explaining while he waited for it to start up. "Radar is a way of detecting distant things, such as airplanes, ships, or in our case, tornadoes. A radar device sends out radio waves, which reflect, or echo, off an object and return to the receiver—that's the dish on the roof. The farther away something is, the longer it takes for the echo to return. So radar can tell us how far something is and in what direction."

"A Doppler radar, like this one, uses the Doppler effect to give us even more information. Remember the trumpets on the train? When they were getting closer, the pitch sounded higher. When they were moving away, it sounded lower."

"The radio waves coming back to us in a Doppler radar work just like those sound waves. If the echo bounces off something that is getting closer, it shifts to a higher frequency. It shifts to a lower frequency if it bounces off something getting farther away. So, Doppler radar can show not only how far away winds and clouds and stuff are, but how they are moving. The computer puts all this information together to show us how fast the tornado is moving, and in what direction."

Zac began typing on the computer's keyboard, and a map appeared on the screen. Most of the map was shaded green. But there was a patch of red, with yellow edges, near the top corner. "That's the supercell," said Zac, pointing. Then he pointed out a small hook shape near the bottom of the red area. "And that's the mesocyclone," he said. "The tornado will be around there."

Every few seconds, the map was updated, as new information came in from the radar receiver. With each update, the supercell moved slowly up the screen.

"We're over here," said Marcus, pointing to a town marked near the middle of the screen. "So it's moving away from us."

"It's heading northeast," said Ning.

"We can take that road," said Lucía. She held a finger to the screen and traced the line of a highway.

Zac nodded. "Let's go and tell Aunt Kim."

Chapter 7
The Pressure Is On

Minutes later, they all set off in Aunt Kim's station wagon. Lucía sat up front next to Aunt Kim. Every few minutes, she tried to get in touch with Jayden on the mobile radio unit. Ning, Zac, and Marcus sat in the back seat. Orbit curled up in the cargo space.

Ning was using her cell phone to track the tornado on the National Weather Service website, but the page seemed to take ages to update.

The weather was calm where they were. There were even patches of blue sky overhead as they turned onto the highway. But to the northeast, where they were headed, the sky was a heavy gray. It was strange to see the golden prairie sunlit beneath the dark sky.

They spoke little as they drove along the nearly empty road. Aunt Kim was worried and in no mood for conversation. Now and then, Lucía would call out to Jayden on the radio. All they heard in return was static.

Orbit started to whine and growl, and Marcus had to calm him.

After a few miles, Aunt Kim braked to a sudden stop. The road ahead was severely damaged. Something had raked a wide cut across it. Brown dirt and gravel showed through deep cracks in the asphalt.

"The tornado must have done this," said Lucía.

"I pray that Jayden wasn't here when it did!" Aunt Kim gulped.

"What's that?" asked Ning, pointing to a small object lying by the roadside.

"I know what it is!" cried Lucía. She jumped out of the car, ran over to it, and picked it up. It was the cone-shaped object she had seen in the back of Shango, Jayden's armored truck. The little cone's metal surface was scarred and dented. Its orange paint was nearly scratched off.

The others joined Lucía, eager to see what she had

found. She explained that she had seen it before in Jayden's truck. Aunt Kim became seriously worried. "So, he was here. But then what could have happened to him? Did he get swallowed up by the twister?" She scanned the landscape, but there were nothing but empty fields in every direction. The only other sign of life was a small house a short distance to the west.

Lucía gave the upper part of the cone a twist. Suddenly, it came away from the base. Attached to the circular base were a number of metal and plastic devices, linked by wires.

"What is all this stuff?" she wondered.

Zac peered at the devices attached to it. "These look like

instruments for recording things—like air pressure, temperature, humidity, and wind speed," he said. "This must be a kind of probe for studying the tornado. I think Jayden placed it here on purpose, in the path of the tornado, to measure conditions inside the twister."

"See, you don't need to worry, Auntie," said Marcus, putting his arm around her. "Jay knew what he was doing. He must have tossed the probe onto the roadside before scrambling out of here."

Aunt Kim still looked worried. "And then what happened to him? Why hasn't he been in touch?"

Marcus could only shrug, as puzzled as everyone else by the uninterrupted static on the radio.

Aunt Kim glanced again at the little house to the west. A narrow road led to it, cutting through the fields from the highway. "I think I'll drive over there and see if there's anyone around who saw him," she said. "Why don't you kids stay here, in case he comes back while I'm gone?"

The station wagon pulled away. Lucía returned her attention to the instruments inside the probe. She studied one of the gauges. "It looks like it recorded a drop in the atmospheric pressure about an hour ago," she said. "It fell by... 100 millibars. Is that a lot?"

Zac's eyebrows shot up. "Yeah, that's huge," he said. "It could only have been caused by a powerful tornado passing overhead."

"You know," said Marcus, "I've never really understood what atmospheric pressure is."

"Come on, Marcus, isn't it obvious?" said Lucía. "It's the weight of the air pressing down all around us."

"I never realized that air weighed anything," said Marcus. He cupped an empty hand and bounced it a few times, trying to feel the weight of the air.

"You're such a weirdo!" smirked Lucía.

"I'm crushed," Marcus said, smiling, "though not, for some reason, by the air."

"Actually, Marcus isn't such a weirdo," said Zac. "For centuries, scientists believed that the air had no weight and did not cause any pressure. It took Evangelista Torricelli to work out that it did."

"Eh vahn jeh LEE stah tawr ih CHEHL ee" Marcus sounded out each syllable. "What an epic name!

"He was a physicist and mathematician born in Italy over 400 years ago," said Zac. "If you're up for it, we could pay him a visit while we're waiting for Aunt Kim."

"We're totally up for it!" said Lucía, who was always ready for another adventure into history.

FLASH!

ZUMMMMMmmmmmmm...

The Backspace app transported the children from the wide Oklahoma prairie to a tiny, cluttered laboratory in 1600's Rome.

The room was crowded with glass and copper bottles, funnels, and tubes. There was barely room for

Zac and his friends to stand.

"This is worse than Jayden's bedroom," muttered Marcus.

Among the clutter stood a small man with long, dark hair and a neat beard. Evangelista Torricelli was pouring a shiny, metallic liquid from a bottle into a tall glass tube.

"What is that stuff you're pouring?" Ning asked.

Torricelli's head jerked up. "What?" he said, startled at the sudden appearance of the visitors. "Ah, you mean this? This is mercury."

"Mercury's pretty toxic," Zac whispered to Ning. "You wouldn't see people doing this sort of experiment today—at least, not without protective gear."

When the tube was full, Torricelli held his thumb over its top and turned it upside down. He placed it in a bowl, also filled with mercury, and removed his thumb. The children watched in silence as mercury ran out of the tube and into the bowl, leaving a gap at the top of the tube. When the gap had reached a few finger-widths

in depth, the mercury stopped flowing out, even though there was plenty still left in the tube.

"Wait, why has it stopped?" Lucía asked. "Why isn't the rest of the mercury flowing out of the tube?"

Torricelli looked up. "Good question, signorina. It is a mystery that has puzzled the greatest thinkers of our age. The answer, they believe, has to do with this gap here at the top of the tube. Where there was mercury, there's now nothing, not even air. I have created a vacuum—an empty space. Most people believe that this vacuum produces some kind of suction, pulling on the mercury and preventing any more of it from leaving the tube. But I am not so sure."

As he said this, Torricelli's smile faded. His cheeks became flushed, and his eyes grew wider.

"What is it?" Lucía asked. "What's wrong?"

"I think he's just had a big idea," said Zac.

Torricelli murmured, "But of course, the vacuum has nothing to do with it. The mercury stopped coming out of the tube because… because of the weight of the air…" The physicist gazed at the surface of the mercury in the bowl. "The weight of the air pushing down on the mercury in the bowl provides enough pressure to keep the rest of the mercury inside the tube!"

Zac tapped the screen of his phone. In a flash, they were back on the Oklahoma roadside.

"Was he right?" gasped Marcus.

"You bet he was!" said Zac. "He was proven right some years later, when someone took Torricelli's mercury tube up a mountain. The height of the mercury in the tube dropped. Who knows why?"

"Because there's less air between the top of a mountain and the top of the atmosphere?" suggested Ning.

"Exactly right!" said Zac. "With less air above, the atmospheric pressure at the mountaintop was lower. The air put less pressure on the mercury in the bowl, allowing more mercury to pour out of the tube. Evangelista Torricelli had invented the mercury barometer—the first device for measuring atmospheric pressure. It's been used by scientists and weather forecasters ever since."

"Why weather forecasters?" asked Marcus.

"Because atmospheric pressure doesn't only change according to how high up you are," said Zac. "It's also affected by the weather. Before a storm, for example, warm, moist air rises to form clouds. The warm, rising air weighs less, causing atmospheric pressure to drop…"

"And when a tornado goes by, it drops by 100 millibars," added Ning.

Zac nodded. "More or less. Tornadoes create giant updrafts, so you get huge drops in pressure."

"You know, I think I'm actually beginning to understand all this!" said Marcus.

"Great!" said Lucía. "Because we're going test you on it later."

Marcus groaned. "Aagh! The pressure!"

Chapter 8

Shango!

The children looked up to see Aunt Kim's car coming back down the road. As she pulled to a stop, Marcus ran up to the window. "Did you find out anything?" he asked.

"I sure did," she said, leaning out the window. "The couple living in the house said they saw a big, armored vehicle drive by about an hour ago, just before the tornado struck. The lady said she saw the driver throw out that orange probe thing and then continue on along the highway. That was the last they saw of him before they went down to their storm shelter."

"It's just like I told you," said Marcus. "Jayden's a pro! He wouldn't have put himself in danger."

"Yeah, but we still don't have any idea what happened to him," said Aunt Kim. "We'll just have to keep looking, I guess." She glanced up at the sky, which had suddenly filled with threatening clouds. At the same time, a wind kicked up and began whipping at their clothes. "You'd better all get in, kids. We've no time to lose."

The car drove on, and the radio continued to pick up only static. Along the way, the children saw more tornado damage—huge trenches torn in cornfields, wrecked fences, and even a toppled windmill. Meanwhile, the darkening sky rumbled with distant thunder. The wind swirled around them, flapping a loose rubber wiper blade against the windshield.

Aunt Kim began muttering to herself, "Where is that boy? … He can't have gone this far…"

"Stop!" yelled Lucía suddenly.

Aunt Kim slammed on the brakes. The tires screeched. Everyone rocked forward in their seats. Poor Orbit nearly ended up in Marcus's lap.

"Back up! Back up!" cried Lucía. "I think I saw Shango."

Aunt Kim put the car into reverse.

"Over there!" said Lucía, pointing.

Sure enough, Jayden's storm-chaser sat a short distance up a dirt track that headed west off the highway. Though it wasn't far from the road, it was hard to see in the dimming light.

"Good eyes, Lucía!" said Aunt Kim. She spun the steering wheel and took off down the track.

The children burst from the station wagon, calling Jayden's name. But to their disappointment, he was nowhere to be found.

"Where could he have gone?" moaned Aunt Kim.

Shango had taken some minor storm damage. The truck's armor was dented and scratched in places. A headlight had been cracked. Otherwise the vehicle looked sound. Moreover, Shango was parked neatly on the side of the track. There was no evidence that Jayden had been in a panic when he left it.

The wind began to strengthen. The light turned an odd yellow color, as it had earlier, outside the garage. Then the hailstones began to fall—big ones.

"Quick! Back in the car!" yelled Aunt Kim, throwing open the door.

"I've just about had my fill of weather today!" complained Marcus once they were safely inside the station wagon. They looked out at the flurry of golfball-sized hailstones crashing down on the hood and windshield. The clatter of hail on the roof was deafening.

"It's like being in the front row of a rock concert during a drum solo," said Lucía.

"More like being inside the drums," said Marcus.

"Look over there!" cried Ning. She was staring out the rear window.

They turned and saw, for the second time that day, a blurry, spinning finger of whirling air snaking out of the bottom of a cloud.

"Another tornado!" wailed Marcus. "And this time it's heading our way."

Aunt Kim restarted the engine and began driving along the track. The twister was off to the north, approaching the highway they'd just left. This track would hopefully take them away from it.

"Let's find somewhere to shelter," said Aunt Kim. Everyone peered out the windows. Even with the headlights on and the wipers at full speed, it was hard to see anything through the downpour.

Then Orbit began to bark.

"It's okay, boy," soothed Zac. "We'll be out of this soon."

But Orbit could not be calmed. His eyes were bright, and his ears pricked up. He continued to yelp and growl.

"I think he senses something," said Lucía. She wiped some moisture from the fogged up window and looked out. "Wait, I see a house up ahead. It's coming up on your left, Aunt Kim."

The shadowy outline of a house appeared through the gloom. Aunt Kim turned the wheel to the left, drove through an open gate, and parked the car in front of a rickety wooden farmhouse.

Lucía reached behind her and hugged Orbit.

"You clever dog! You found us some shelter!"

Orbit panted and barked some more. He still seemed unusually excited about something.

"Wait here, everyone, while I go and speak to the owners," said Kim. She opened the door, pulled her coat up over her head, and made a dash for the porch.

Orbit leapt over the seats in an attempt to follow her. Zac had to grab him by the collar and slam the door shut. "What's got into you, boy? Calm down!" he scolded.

The children watched as Kim knocked on the front door. They waited hopefully, but after several minutes, it was clear no one was home.

Kim returned to the car and leaned in. "I saw the entrance to a storm cellar around the side of the house. I'm sure the owners won't mind if we wait out the storm down there."

The children piled out of the car and hurried after

Aunt Kim. She led them to a heavy wooden door set at an angle into the sloping ground. Aunt Kim hauled the door open. She ushered the children one by one down wooden steps that led to the cellar.

Once everyone was inside, Aunt Kim took a final glance at the sky. The tornado, now much closer, was a whirling, thundering brown cloud, churning its way through the fields toward them. She prayed that wherever Jayden was, he was safe. Then she stepped inside and pulled the door closed behind her.

Chapter 9
Tornado in a Bottle

Ning found a light switch near the top of the stairs. It turned on a bare light bulb hanging from the ceiling. The bulb lit up the bare brick walls of the shelter. The children had half expected to find the house's owners taking shelter, but nobody was there.

In the middle of the room there were a table and some chairs. There were boxes on the floor filled with old children's toys. In the far corner, there was a sink, a refrigerator, and a microwave and a shelf piled with plates and cups.

"Hey, we could really make ourselves at home down here," said Marcus. "I wonder if there's any food in that refrigerator."

"We're not taking any of their food," scolded Aunt Kim. "You can help yourselves to some water, if you're thirsty."

"Where's Orbit?" Zac suddenly asked.

Everyone looked around for the dog. He was nowhere to be seen.

"He must still be outside!" Lucía gasped.

"I don't understand what's gotten into that dog," said Zac, running back up the steps. "He's always right at my side. I'm going out to find him."

"No!" cried Aunt Kim as Zac pushed against the heavy, slanted door. A screaming wind blew in through the gap. Zac staggered backward. The door fell shut with a loud bang.

"That tornado could be right over us by now!" said Kim.

Zac reluctantly returned to the cellar.

Lucía put a comforting arm around his shoulder. "Orbit's a smart dog," she reassured him. "I'm sure he's found shelter somewhere, probably in the crawl space under the house."

Aunt Kim and the children tried to find a board game to help pass the time, and to distract themselves from their worries. They rummaged through the boxes, but found little beyond dolls, wooden toys, some fancy dress costumes, and a tube of silver-colored glitter.

The glitter gave Zac an idea. "Anybody want to make a tornado in a bottle?" he asked.

"Haven't we had enough tornadoes for one day?" moaned Marcus.

"I think it's a great idea," said Ning.

Zac took an empty plastic water bottle from his backpack. He filled it about three-quarters full with water from the faucet. Then he added a few drops of dish soap from a bottle he found near the sink. Finally, he dropped a few pinches of glitter into the water bottle. He screwed the cap back on tightly.

"Now, look at this," he said to the others.

They all watched closely as Zac turned the bottle upside down, holding it by the neck. He took hold of the bottle's base with his other hand, and gave it a spin. It spun for a few seconds before Zac stopped it by grabbing hold of the base.

The water inside the bottle continued to swirl, and everyone saw that it had formed a rapidly spinning

whirlpool. The glitter made the twisting cone easier to see.

"It looks like a tornado!" said Aunt Kim. "And much prettier than the big one up there!"

The kids took turns twirling the bottle, competing to see who could create the strongest twister. Even Aunt Kim took a turn. Distracted from their worries, they quickly lost track of time.

Suddenly, the door to the cellar creaked open. Everyone jumped up startled, not sure whether to expect an angry tornado or the owners of the house returning home. Instead, they were overjoyed to see Jayden's face grinning down at them. Behind him, bright sunlight poured from a blue sky. The storm had passed.

Orbit shot between Jayden's legs and came flying down the steps, barking excitedly. Zac hugged him with joy and relief.

"Hey y'all, it's great to see you, but what are you doing in here?" Jayden asked. He followed Orbit down the stairs at a calmer pace.

"You fool, Jay, we came to rescue you!" scolded his mother as she hugged him.

"Rescue me?" cried Jayden. "Why, that's sweet of you, but I don't need any rescuing. You shouldn't have risked your necks coming out and trying."

"We were worried, Jay," said Marcus. "We couldn't get through to you on the radio."

Jay nodded. "Yeah, sorry about that, cuz. I had a few technical problems."

"Why did you abandon Shango, Jay?" Aunt Kim wanted to know.

"It's kind of embarrassing to admit, ma, but… well, see… I sort of ran out of gas."

They all laughed. "Mr. Professional Storm-Chaser ran out of gas." Aunt Kim smiled. "So that was your technical problem, huh? Well, luckily I filled the spare can at the gas station, so we can refuel Shango… But why didn't you just radio us and let us know, Jay?"

"The radio was in Shango, and I was forced to leave it because the twister was approaching. It was an EF3, and that can…"

"Lift cars into the air, we know," said Lucía.

"Exactly, so I had to find shelter someplace else. There's an old storm shelter by the side of the track. I decided to wait out the tornado in there. Eventually, it passed. I was about to head back to Shango when another big twister arrived, and I was forced back into the shelter. The next thing I knew, Orbit showed up. Man, you can't imagine how surprised I was! I couldn't figure out how he got so far from home."

"That explains why Orbit was going so crazy in the car!" said Lucía. "He must have smelled you or something."

"Either that dog has a magical sense of smell, or you need a shower, son!" laughed Aunt Kim.

"Maybe I do," nodded Jayden. "Anyway, when the storm cleared, it was Orbit who led me here to you all."

"You're an incredible dog!" said Ning, patting Orbit.

"He sure is," agreed Jayden.

That evening, Aunt Kim cooked out to celebrate their survival of the day's adventures unharmed. Everyone sat around the picnic table in Aunt Kim's back yard. They enjoyed the warm early evening sunshine as they ate, drank, and talked. Hamburgers and hot dogs

sizzled on the grill. Above, the sky was a beautiful deep blue.

"I can hardly believe there were two tornadoes today," said Ning. "Everything's so peaceful now."

"That's the weather for you," said Zac. "It's always changing."

Jayden listened to his portable radio while he ate. Suddenly, he frowned. "Oh no!"

"What is it, Jay?" asked Kim, concerned.

"It's the weather forecast," said Jayden. "Bad news! Nothing but clear skies and calm weather for the next few days. It's gonna be dull, dull, dull!"

"Dull is good," smiled Marcus, chomping into another hamburger. "I have no problem with dull!"

Meet the Scientists

James Pollard Espy

James Pollard Espy (1785–1860), nicknamed the Storm King, was an American *meteorologist* (weather scientist) who made important advances in the study of storms.

William Charles Redfield

The American meteorologist William Redfield (1789–1857) was one of the first people to propose that hurricanes are large and powerful storms of swirling air. He was an outspoken opponent of James Espy's ideas.

Vilhelm and Jacob Bjerknes

Father and son Vilhelm (1862–1951) and Jacob (1897–1975) Bjerknes (*bih AIRK nehs*) of Norway helped found the science of weather forecasting. Jacob had ideas about how cyclones form and die out and introduced the idea of weather fronts.

John Park Finley

The American meteorologist and army officer John Park Finley (1854–1943) pioneered the scientific study of tornadoes.

Ernest Fawbush and Robert Miller

Ernest J. Fawbush and Robert C. Miller (1920-1998) were U.S. Air Force weather officers, who, on March 25, 1948, made the first successful tornado forecast in recorded history.

Ted Fujita

Tetsuya "Ted" Fujita (1920–1998) was a Japanese American scientist who studied severe storms. He introduced the Fujita scale for classifying tornadoes.

Christian Doppler

Christian Doppler (1803–1853), an Austrian mathematician and physicist, explained the change in pitch heard when the source of a noise is getting closer or farther away. This change became known as the Doppler effect.

Evangelista Torricelli

Evangelista Torricelli *(tawr ih CHEHL ee)* (1608–1647) was an Italian mathematician and physicist. He invented the barometer and made important discoveries in *optics* (the study of light) and in the mathematics of infinity.

Glossary

air mass a body of air with uniform temperature and humidity

atmospheric pressure the weight of the overlying air pressing down all around

barometer an instrument for measuring atmospheric pressure

condense to change from a gas (or vapor) to a liquid

cumulonimbus a low-altitude cloud forming a towering mass with a flat base and often a wide top, associated with storms

cyclone a system of winds rotating inward to an area of low pressure

humidity the amount of water vapor, or moisture, in the atmosphere

mercury a heavy, silvery-white metal that is liquid at room temperature

mesocyclone a rotating air mass associated with a supercell, which can produce a tornado

meteorology the study of the atmosphere to forecast the weather

millibar one-thousandth of a bar, a unit of atmospheric pressure

radar a system for detecting distant objects by sending out radio waves that echo from the object and return to the source

selfie an informal self-portrait, usually taken with a cell phone

simulator a machine designed to provide a realistic imitation of something

supercell a large, slow-moving area of up- and downdrafts, which causes violent storms, including tornadoes

updraft an upward movement of air

vacuum a space empty of matter

vapor the gaseous form of a substance

virtual created and existing only in a computer—like the historical scenes visited in Zac's Backspace app

wall cloud a cloud mass that forms beneath a cumulonimbus. Tornadoes can form from a wall cloud.

Additional Resources

Books

Hurricanes & Tornadoes (Physical & Human Geography)
Joanna Brundle (Book Life, 2017)

Investigating Tornadoes (Edge Books: Investigating Natural Disasters)
Elizabeth Elkins (Raintree, 2018)

Storm Chasing (Xtreme Adventure)
S. L. Hamilton (Abdo & Daughters, 2014)

Tornadoes (Library of Natural Disasters)
Neil Morris (World Book, 2018)

Websites

National Geographic – Tornadoes: The Science Behind the Destruction
https://news.nationalgeographic.com/news/2014/04/140430-tornadoes-meteorology-atmospheric-science-disasters/

This website explains how twisters form, where and when they strike, and the difficulties of forecasting them.

National Weather Service – Tornado Awareness
https://www.weather.gov/cae/tornado.html

Information about tornadoes, their size, strength, and speed, where they most frequently occur, and what to do if threatened by one.

Weather Wiz Kids
http://www.weatherwizkids.com/

A website all about weather, with pages about different kinds of weather, including tornadoes, as well as weather forecasting and suggestions for experiments.

Index